Bearded Dragons

Written by Jessica Lee Anderson

Photos by David Kenny

Paperback ISBN: 978-1-964078-18-2

To Jim, Marilyn, Maddy, and Jimmy—thanks for sharing Dirk with us. - JLA

To my wife Heather, my daughter Madison, and my parents Peter and Edel. - DK

We would like to thank the following:

Hudson Valley Reptile & Rescue: A reptile rescuer and educator, Brian Parkhurst has been passing on his knowledge of reptiles through educational programs for 22 years. Brian works hard to find homes for reptiles that are surrendered to the rescue. HVR&R is located in Saugerties, New York. https://www.hvreptilerescue.org

Ocean Gallery II Fish and Reptiles: A small, local, family operated pet store in North Plainfield, New Jersey, run by Craig Ost who has over 30 years of experience in reptile keeping. They also specialize in saltwater fish and corals. https://www.oceangallery22.com/

If you are looking to bring a bearded dragon into your family, please consider a reptile rescue or local reptile store that works with reputable breeders. Bringing any reptile into your home is a lifelong commitment.

All photos taken by David Kenny apart from P.6: Jessica Lee Anderson (nested image of Dirk) and P. 34: Michael Anderson and Madison Kenny

Bearded dragons, called beardies for short, are one of the most popular lizards in the world! These reptiles get their name because they are armored in scales like dragons, and they have a throat pouch under their chin that looks like a spiky beard.

Both male and female bearded dragons have beards with thorn-like spikes. Beardies can puff up their beards to look larger or more intimidating if they feel threatened or stressed. This is a natural bearded dragon defense mechanism.

Beardies will also flare out their throat pouch to remove old, itchy skin. Like all reptiles, bearded dragons will shed their skin throughout their entire lives, especially as they grow. (They even shed skin from their nostrils!)

Bearded dragon skin is made of keratin, the same material as your hair and nails. Their spikes can feel rough yet flexible. When beardies puff up, the spikes become sharper, but they are not dangerous.

Bearded dragon beards may turn black when they puff up their necks. Their black beards can indicate that they are feeling stressed, aggressive, or sick. Their beards may also turn black when trying to impress a potential mate.

Beardies may also turn darker while basking. Darker pigments absorb more heat, meaning they will warm up quicker. Beardies may also change colors to blend into their environment (camouflage) to avoid predators and sneak up on prey.

Bearded dragons communicate in other ways besides puffing out their beards and changing colors. They will do push-ups to display dominance or to impress a mate. They will also bob their heads as a sign of aggression, dominance, or excitement.

If they sense a threat or feel intimidated, bearded dragons may wave a front leg as a sign of submission. This indicates to others that they don't want to fight. Small, younger bearded dragons may wave more often than older, larger beardies as they are more vulnerable.

All reptiles are "cold-blooded," meaning their body temperature varies (though biologists use the technical term poikilothermic instead). In the wild, beardies live in areas like woodlands, savannahs, and deserts. They often bask on rocks or branches because the sun raises their body temperature.

In captivity, a beardie needs a large enough enclosure, a basking lamp to stay warm, a UVB lamp for proper bone development, climbing branches, and spots to hide and cool off if needed. Following care guides, offering enrichment, and receiving care from an exotic veterinarian can keep pet bearded dragons happy and healthy.

Some people debate whether there are eight or nine species of bearded dragons. They are all native to Australia and fall in the genus *Pogona*. Central (or inland) bearded dragons are the easiest to recognize as they are the most numerous species worldwide. Central bearded dragons are native to the central part of Australia.

Bearded dragons are in the family of agamid lizards (Agamidae). Agamid lizards have distinct habitats and unique teeth, plus they don't lose their tails as a defense mechanism like some other kinds of lizards. (For example, some geckos might drop their tails if they sense danger.)

In the wild, bearded dragons are semi-arboreal, meaning they spend time in the trees or shrubs, though they mostly dwell on land (terrestrial). Beardies are natural climbers! They climb to seek food, bask, survey the area, and escape predators.

Bearded dragon tails can be long—even over half their body length! Beardies use their tails to stay balanced when they hunt, climb, or run. They will often hold their tails up when they are alert. While their tails don't fall off naturally, they can be affected by injuries, infections, or disease.

Beardies have five toes on every foot. Their back feet each have an exceptionally long toe that helps them climb up and down various surfaces. Pet bearded dragons might need their nails trimmed to prevent scratches and getting caught on things like fabrics (which can cause toe injuries).

Unlike humans, beardies do not have protective discs in their spines. This means that they can sustain spinal injuries if they fall from a high distance or someone drops them. While they are hardy lizards overall, it is important to be careful handling them.

Wild bearded dragons vary in color and patterns, often blending into their native environment. Pet bearded dragons have been selectively bred to have genetic variations called morphs. They can be different sizes, colors, patterns, and textures (such as the leatherback morph that has smaller scales and a smoother back).

Look at these examples of various beardie colors and patterns!

Beardies have excellent eyesight! They have a wide field of vision given the placement of their eyes on the sides of their head—useful for finding food and avoiding predators in the wild. Beardies will tilt their heads to look at something right in front of them, making it seem like they are giving a serious case of "side-eye."

Parietal eye

Bearded dragons have a special light-sensitive organ on the top of their heads between their eyes called a parietal eye (sometimes referred to as a "third eye"). The parietal eye can detect changes in light and shadows, beneficial for avoiding predators. This is why some pet beardies might get startled or reactive if they get picked up from overhead.

Ear

Bearded dragons have good hearing, and they can even recognize voices. Loud sounds, rumblings, and vibrations can be bothersome to certain beardies. Their ears look like holes on the sides of their heads. Similar to you, they have middle ear and inner ear parts that allow them to hear.

Nostril

Like you, beardies breathe through their nostrils. They sometimes gape with their mouths open to regulate temperature, like a dog panting. Bearded dragons have difficulty breathing when flipped on their backs because their weight compresses their lungs. They can also be sensitive to smoke, chemicals, and strong smells.

Beardies have teeth fused to their jawbone (acrodont teeth) and replaceable teeth at the front (pleurodont teeth). Anything with a mouth can bite, though beardies are generally docile and only bite as a last resort if they feel threatened. They might nibble as a feeding response (for example, biting at berry-looking painted fingernails).

Beardies are omnivores, meaning they eat both meat and plants. They have venom glands, but their spit is a concern for prey rather than people. Beardies have strong enough jaws that they can crush insects with hard shells! They need a well-balanced diet with fresh daily greens like mustard greens and collard greens.

Like other kinds of reptiles, bearded dragons have forked tongues. They have a sensory organ on the roof of their mouth called the Jacobson's organ that picks up smells. This provides beardies with information about the environment, food, and other animals in the area. Their tongues are short and sticky—perfect for catching insects and other meals.

Just like you, beardies enjoy treats (although you likely don't think hornworms are tasty)! Adult bearded dragons have different dietary needs than growing, young beardies. Adults need more plants and fewer insects, and they may eat less often. Certain food items like citrus, onions, garlic, avocado, and more can make bearded dragons sick. It is important to research safe, healthy food options.

Bearded dragons have a need for dietary calcium throughout their lives, especially when they are young with bones that are developing. Without proper nutrition, supplements, and UVB lighting, beardies can develop metabolic bone disease (MBD for short) that can cause bone and teeth deformities.

Bearded dragons reproduce by laying eggs, about 16-24 in a clutch on average. A female bearded dragon can lay up to 4 clutches in a year. In about two months, healthy beardies will use an "egg tooth" to poke a hole in the egg, a process called pipping. They will hatch out of the egg at their own speed, usually about a day or two later. (The "egg tooth" falls off soon after and will be replaced by a regular tooth.)

As bearded dragons start to grow, they can become territorial and defensive. Bearded dragons are solitary animals by nature, so housing them together can lead to stress, fights, and injuries. When it comes to people, beardies can be friendly, curious, and even cuddly if they are well taken care of and shown kindness, patience, and gentleness.

Wild bearded dragons live between 4 to 10 years, but they can live longer in captivity with proper care. Studies have shown these lizards are intelligent! Researchers observed how bearded dragons learn by repetition, observation, and imitating others. Given their smarts, friendly personalities, and unique looks, it is no surprise why beardies are so popular!

Jessica Lee Anderson is an award-winning author of over 75 books for young readers including the NAOMI NASH chapter book series and many nonfiction books about reptiles. Jessica loves spending time in nature and exploring the outdoors with her husband, Michael, and their daughter, Ava! Jessica and her family enjoy beardie sitting for friends. You can learn more about Jessica by visiting www.jessicaleeanderson.com.

David Kenny is a photographer from New Jersey who enjoys photographing a wide variety of subjects, including reptiles, amphibians, birds, mammals, and landscapes. His images have been published in numerous books, magazines, calendars, and articles. Dave would like to thank Bill DiMuccio, Craig Ost, and Brian Parkhurst.

Want to learn more about reptiles? Check out these books:

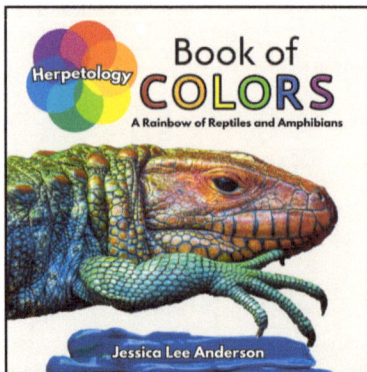

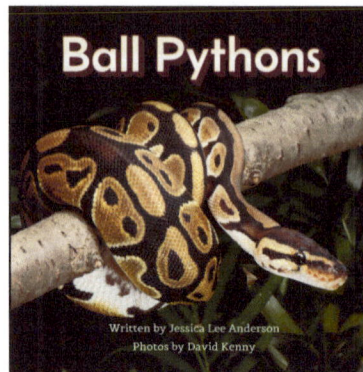

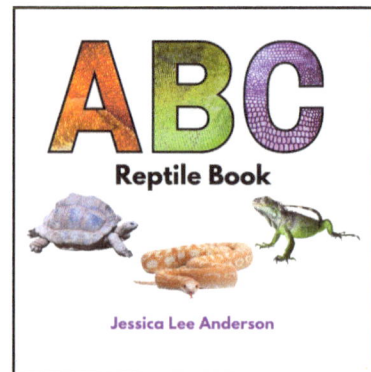

Herpetology Book of COLORS
A Rainbow of Reptiles and Amphibians
Jessica Lee Anderson

Ball Pythons
Written by Jessica Lee Anderson
Photos by David Kenny

ABC Reptile Book
Jessica Lee Anderson